The Book of Shadows

A JOURNAL OF
MAGICK, SPELLS, & RITUALS

ANASTASIA GREYWOLF

wellfleet
press

Contents

How to Use This Journal

Depictions of witches and covens are as diverse and vast as how witchcraft is practiced around the world. When the word "spells" is mentioned, our cultural echelon has us default to conjure up witchy rhyming incantations using words like "hocus pocus" and "bubble, bubble, toil and trouble" or images of black cauldrons and cruel, older women with giant moles and pallid skin. In fact, witches are sometimes mistakenly associated with darkness or evil, but the truth is actually quite different. Since truth lies in darkness sometimes, shadows do not have to be something dark and sinister but rather hidden—hence the title of this journal, *The Book of Shadows*. Traditionally, a Book of Shadows serves as a diary for magick, or a book of records for a witch's magick and rituals. It is a place where you can record dreams, spells, and outcomes.

There are many different types of witches and witchcraft. For instance, some view the practice of witchcraft as a skillset while others view it as a religion. This broad variance makes witchcraft incredibly accessible. Those who practice can do so alone, or with covens or groups, should they prefer. Some of the different types of witchcraft include:

★ Ceremonial witchcraft means practitioners perform spells strictly by the book and focus on expert execution of rituals and ceremonies.

★ Eclectic witchcraft is just as the word suggests, a mixed bag of practices and traditions.

★ Solitary witchcraft is suited for readers of this journal since solitary witches operate alone.

A big part of witchcraft is intent. If you go forward with the spells and incantations in this journal, it is important to have the purest intent. Energy is all around us. Sometimes, unbidden, we can have negative effects on ourselves or others if our thoughts run away into reflections on harm or negativity. I recommend that you do some quiet meditation, finding focus and a positive mindset, before beginning spells. This will help cleanse the mind and prepare the soul. At the center of positive witchery is white light.

Spell casting comes from within, which means the most essential tool needed is you, with complete clarity. Without the right frame of mind, connecting to positive energies and higher powers will be fruitless endeavors.

The Difference Between Magic and Magick

The word "magick" was created by Aleister Crowley, the founder and occultist of the Thelema religion. He added the "k" to distinguish his craft from illusionists and magicians since he did not perform "tricks."

Journal Organization

This journal is a combination of spells that you can practice with common items you may already have or that can easily be found online or at local stores along with journal prompts to both record and reflect on your spellwork.

Spells and Rituals

The purpose of the spells and rituals in this journal is to help propel those with positive intentions toward their goals. These spells and rituals can be utilized by anyone at any practicing level and are meant to bring harmony, emotional peace, well-being, and overall positivity to your life.

The Difference Between Rituals and Spells

While a ritual can have a spell attached to it, rituals are usually events that celebrate, honor, or are performed as a rite of passage. Rituals are many times repeated annually, monthly, or lunarly (see page 22) and can be performed by an individual or a group. A spell is about directing energy toward a specific goal, helping to manifest a specific outcome.

Customizations and Sidebars

Some spells offer customizations that will help you, as the caster, to intimately connect more to the spell and therefore be more efficient at producing the desired results. In addition, sidebars in some spells provide an extra layer of resources or examples to expand upon the spells.

Spell Notes

The spell note section is a place to record the details of your spellwork, such as the date, time of day, and moon phase that you performed a spell, and is a designed space to write any notes, modifications, or special points (was is it successful or not?) to remember for when you repeat a spell.

Writing Prompts

The writing prompts aide in meditation and also in manifestation of spells. The purpose of the prompts are to bring focus to the spellcaster. Your mindset is the foundation to your intentions, and intentions are the baseline to spell casting. In this journal, we want you to take a deep dive into your perspective and explore your inner workings to gain clarity. For with clarity comes efficient spellwork.

This Journal's Intention

While this journal offers spells, its core purpose is to help casters engage in practices that can lead to spiritual clarity. The journaling aspect is meant to offer support as well as to serve as a learning tool, be it for those who are just starting out or those who are a bit more seasoned.

Witchcraft Essentials

Before getting started, there are some basic tools and materials to have on hand. In this section, we will look at how to create a tool kit and the importance of colors, herbs, and crystals to better prepare you for spellwork. Many items can be found around your house or at local stores. For those that are a bit less common, they are pretty easy to find online. There are even sites and shops that sell bundles like Etsy.com. If you're new to practicing witchcraft, here is a list of essentials to help you get started. Each item is explained in further detail.

Spell Candles

Herbs

Crystals and Stones

Consecrated Water

Smudge Sticks

Chalice

Burning Bowl (or Cauldron)

Essential Oils

Altar

Athame, Knife, or Blade

Wand

Pendulum

Coarse Salt or Sea Salt

Incense

Spell Candles, Colors, and Their Meanings

Spell candles are candles designated for spells and are sometimes anointed (if the spell calls for it). A set of spell candles in a variety of colors is good to keep on hand for spells and rituals—and having them decorate your altar is a bonus. The good thing about candles is that they come in a variety of shapes and sizes. If you're running low on space, tea candles are recommended. If you're buying new candles, try to find ones made of soy wax, as they're better for the environment, produce less soot, and burn more slowly. Because candles can be integral to many spells, each candle color has a particular meaning.

WHITE: Spirituality, peace, higher self, purity

GRAY/SILVER: Intuition, psychism, dreams, femininity, true moon

GOLD: Wealth, masculinity, luck, power, happiness, the sun

YELLOW: Intelligence, learning, reason, focus, memory, joy

ORANGE: Business, success, justice, ambition, opportunity, celebration

PINK: Self-love, nurturing, friendship, romantic love, caring, emotional healing

PURPLE: Abilities, influence, authority, wisdom, hidden knowledge, psychism

BLUE: Travel, communication, calm, creativity, forgiveness, inspiration

GREEN: Growth, nature, nurture, fertility, abundance, money, healing, renewal

BLACK: Protection, banishing, binding, anti-negativity

Herbs

Herbs usually play an integral role in spellwork. Here are the most commonly used herbs for spell casting to keep on hand.

LAVENDER: Used to enhance clarity and protection, bring love, and encourage fertility.

MUGWORT: Used for the enhancement of dreams and divination.

MINT: Used to lure love, ward off evil, enhance wellness, and draw in money.

ROSEMARY: Used typically in protection and love spells.

Crystals and Stones

Crystals and stones have many uses: to facilitate healing, serve as protective talismans, or even be worn as pieces of jewelry. They can be used as markings, for building sacred circles, for wands, and more. Here are some of the most commonly used crystals and stones that you should keep in your tool kit.

AMBER: This fossilized tree sap is associated with the sun due to its coloring. It's often utilized in protection spells.

CITRINE: Citrine is a type of powerful quartz known for cleansing abilities and psychic enhancement.

AMETHYST: This stone is particularly useful for dreams and deep meditation.

CLEAR QUARTZ: This is the most versatile of the crystals, and it's definitely the one to have if nothing else. Clear quartz serves as a booster for other materials and herbs and can be used for meditation, protection, and focus.

BLOODSTONE: Despite the name, this green stone with red accents is associated with health, success, good luck, and courage.

MALACHITE: It's typically used for prosperity magick, warding off evil, and protection.

OBSIDIAN: This black crystal boosts strength and can be used in banishing magick. Obsidian is said to be sacred to Hecate, the goddess of witches.

ROSE QUARTZ: Perfect for spells pertaining to love, emotion, and relationships, rose quartz is great for bringing peace and diffusing tense energy.

MOONSTONE: Ruled by the moon, this stone boosts intuition and dream recall, supports women's health, and calms emotions. Moonstone can be used as a substitute for rose quartz or amethyst.

TIGER'S EYE: Used to promote courage, good fortune, strength, and self-confidence, tiger's eye can also be carried around as a good luck charm.

Consecrated Water

Some spells or rituals call for consecrated water. There are a couple of ways to do this with the aid of moonlight.

INSTRUCTIONS

1. Leave a cup of water outside in the moonlight for three nights in a row: before, during, and after the full moon.

2. Leave a cup of water outside during a full moon. Drop a piece of silver (a coin, a piece of jewelry, etc.) into it. Leave it overnight, allowing the moonlight to bless the water. The next morning, remove the silver and store the water in a glass bottle. This water will be good to use until the next full moon.

Smudge Sticks and Smudging

A smudge stick is a bundled wad of dried herbs that is rolled (usually tied) together and is burned to cleanse a space, ward off negative energy, or begin a spell or ritual. Smudging is part of many traditions. Smudge sticks are also known as bundles. There are many types of smudge sticks that can be used in spellwork.

The act of smudging is an ancient ritual in which a person takes a smudge stick, or herb bundle, burns it and directs the smoke around an object, person, or space. A great quality of smudging is that you can smudge as much as you want, whenever you like. Smudging with a sage stick is quick and easy. Simply hold the smoldering stick over your burning bowl (or cauldron, see below) and hold the item you wish to cleanse over the smoke. Hold your intention of clearing previous energy from the item and direct your own onto it. Be sure to smudge the room both before and after this process to keep the energy of the space clear. Below are some other common herbs used for smudging:

CEDAR: This is used for blessing new homes, driving out negative energy, and bringing in positive influences.

JUNIPER: Invigorating the body and mind, juniper is often burned for purification during rituals.

LAVENDER: Also used for cleansing, lavender can manifest the energy of healing, tranquility, and happiness.

MUGWORT: This is best used for dream stimulation, though it can also be used to clear negative energy and cleansing.

PALO SANTO: This herb inspires creativity and works on clearing negative energy.

ROSEMARY: While the herb itself is commonly used in spells, a rosemary smudge stick is also good for spellwork. It acts as a cleanser not only for your home but also your aura.

WHITE SAGE: This is the best- known smudge plant. It works well to alter the energy in a room, purifying and cleansing the space. White Sage is sacred to some Native American practices and due to over-harvesting the plant is endangered. When possible see alternative herbs.

Burning Bowl (or Cauldron)

A burning bowl, or cauldron, is one of the most important items you should have since many spells call for burning incense, herbs, and paper, which makes a fireproof burning bowl an essential item. It can be made of stone, cast iron, copper, abalone seashell, or other fireproof material. Some burning bowls and cauldrons can double as a chalice,  another item that is also needed for an altar (see page 13). Typically, either a burning bowl or a chalice is chosen for an altar, but if you wish to have both, that is also fine.

Chalice

Also referred to as a cup or goblet, a chalice has several uses in spells and rituals, such as offering libations. It can stand empty or be utilized as a symbol or to hold an ingredient.

Flower Essences

While flower essences and essential oils are both extracted from plants and flowers, how they are extracted are very different. Flower essences are soaked in water, then they are either boiled or placed in sunlight to extract the flower's unique "essence" and energy, filtered, and preserved in alcohol. Plant and flower essences have little to no scent and are used as a homeopathic remedy. Since most flower essences contain a little bit of alcohol from the distillation process, be sure to read the manufacturer's ingredients carefully before using or choose an alcohol-free flower essence.

SAFETY NOTE: *Some flower essences can be harmful to pregnant and breast-feeding women and pets or can cause allergic reactions. Check with your doctor before using them.*

Essential Oils

Essentials oils are very potent extracts that are made from taking the leaves, plant, bark, or flower and then distilling, steaming, or pressing them to extract their "essential" oils that create their fragrances. Essential oils are used for different therapeutic practices, such as aromatherapy. The use of essential oils in spells and rituals is a universal practice. Essential oils can serve many purposes, such as enhancing a spell or blended with a carrier oil for anointing objects or people (see page 14). Essential oils can also be used in a diffuser to help purify your space. Because essential oils are extremely concentrated, they can burn and should NEVER be directly applied to the skin, body, or ingested. They must first be mixed and diluted with a carrier oil before being applied to the body. Read the manufacturer's label carefully for the dilution percentages between drops of essential oils and carrier oils that are safe for adults.

SAFETY NOTE: *Never ingest essential oils or place them directly onto your body or skin. They are highly poisonous and can burn or can cause allergic reactions. Essential oils must be mixed with a carrier oil and then applied to the body. Essential oils should not be used by children, older adults, pregnant and breastfeeding women, or pets. Check with your doctor before using them.*

Carrier Oils

Carrier oils (also known as base oils) are used to dilute essential oils and to "carry" them to your skin. Carrier oils are usually made from nut-based plants. Remember, always mix essential oils with a carrier oil before applying to the body. Read the manufacturer's label carefully for the dilution percentages between drops of essential oils and carrier oils that are safe for adults. Examples of carrier oils include:

olive oil
jojoba oil
sunflower oil
avocado oil
grapeseed oil
coconut oil

sweet almond oil
black seed oil
argan oil
hazelnut oil
hemp oil
sesame oil
apricot kernel oil

When using any oil, keep in mind if you have allergies (such as a nut allergy) in addition to your skin type and where you'll be applying the oil mixture. If oil is to be applied to your skin, experiment first and do a patch test to see how your skin responds.

Oil Blends

While you can certainly buy premade oil blends from vendors, it's fairly simple to make them yourself and more cost-efficient. As with all oils, make sure you keep your intent in mind as you mix them. Here are some popular oil blends that can be used with spells and meditation throughout this journal. When making your own oil blends, be sure to ALWAYS blend essential oils with a carrier oil.

Van-Van Oil Blend

Derived from Hoodoo practices, Van-Van is a multi-purpose oil blend used for anointing, removing negativity, cleansing, attracting positivity, banishing, and as a lucky handwash. It can charge and empower amulets and talismans, be used as a perfume, or be used in rituals to cleanse bad energy.

INGREDIENTS

2-ounce (60 ml) glass bottle with dropper
2 tablespoons (30 ml) of preferred carrier oil
5 drops lemongrass essential oil
5 drops citronella essential oil
1 drop palmarosa essential oil
1 drop vetivert essential oil
Pinch of dried lemongrass
Pyrite (fool's gold)

Blend the oils together well, then place into a container with a lid. Let the oil mixture sit in a dark place for a week. Once complete, stir in a couple of pinches (depending on how much essential oil you used) of dried lemongrass, followed by a few pyrite pieces. Place the oil blend into the glass bottle, and your Van-Van Oil Blend is good to go. Store in a dark, cool place.

Protection Oil Blend

This oil blend can be used to protect against magical attacks and create psychic protection for your property (home, car, etc.) or for people you wish to keep safe. Be sure to keep your intent clear as you blend the oils.

INGREDIENTS

2-ounce (60 ml) glass bottle with dropper
2 tablespoons (30 ml) almond oil (or preferred carrier oil)
3 drops lavender essential oil
3 drops rose essential oil
1 drop hyssop essential oil
Pinch of dried basil

INSTRUCTIONS

Blend the oils together well, then stir in a couple of pinches of dried basil. Place the oil blend into the glass bottle. Store in a dark, cool place.

Anointing Oil Blend

Plain, cold-pressed extra virgin olive oil is perfect for the purposes of anointing. The addition of the essential oils below (in addition to calamus, cassia, or cinnamon) can add a fragrant smell and are mentioned in religious texts.

INGREDIENTS

2-ounce (60 ml) glass bottle with dropper
2 tablespoons (30 ml) cold-pressed extra virgin olive oil
6 drops of myrrh essential oil
6 drops of frankincense essential oil

INSTRUCTIONS

Carefully pour the extra virgin olive oil into the bottle. Using an eyedropper, add the essential oils to the bottle. If you feel comfortable without the aid of a religious authority, say a prayer over the oil to bless it. This should be said firmly and in good faith.

PRAYER

Air, Earth, Fire, and Wind,

I pray to thee to anoint this oil.

Cleanse it of any defilement in or upon it.

Make it pure for this work.

So mote it be.

Altar

Altars can be used for magick and spell casting, meditation, worship, setting new intentions, rituals, and even yoga. Altars are meant to be sacred and can be as simple or as extravagant as you deem fit. Altars bear the personality of their creators, so be sure to make your altar authentically you. There is no right or wrong way to create an altar. On the next page you'll find some points to keep in mind when creating your altar.

* Choose a surface for your altar. Altars can be almost anywhere in your home from tabletops to window ledges, or even inside of a cupboard. Some witches make their altars from the ground up with large pieces of wood or glass. Be creative (using a basket or large cookie tin) or mundane (a shoebox or storage cr ate). It can be as big or as small as you want, whatever makes the most sense to you.

* Positioning can be important. Many people prefer to place their altars facing north, or east, or they choose a position based on the elements. Some ignore this entirely, but if you want to use a cardinal point, here are their corresponding elements:

North = earth
South = fire
East = air
West = water

* Next, choose your sacred objects. If you find that you have to buy certain items, be sure to cleanse them first because they could be carrying negative energy. And if you happen upon a new item down the road, long after you've made your altar, it's okay to add things whenever you wish. An altar can be altered at will!

* A piece of cloth or fabric is usually used as the base of an altar (it also serves as a creative way to conceal an ugly table or transform a cardboard box). Many people choose a fabric in their favorite color or a color that makes them feel uplifted, but you can use anything. Using what suits you is a running theme when it comes to altar making.

* Crystals, minerals, and rocks of different kinds should be represented on your altar. But if you're new to witchcraft, simply choose one that you feel especially drawn to, maybe because of its color or shape. Having even one stone will help tie your altar together.

* Due to their living and "breathing" nature, live plants are recommended for altars. Plants symbolize grounding and vitality. Dried herbs and spices are also typically used and great for altars,

but if you want to grow a basil plant, for example, it can serve as a twofer for your altar.

★ There are other things that can be added to altars, such as drawings, jewelry, money, statues, and more. Whatever you add, and this cannot be stressed enough, make sure it speaks to you.

Spiritual Cleanse Before Continuing

Before reading further in this journal, please partake in the following mental and spiritual cleanse. While it's recommended to start this journal with the cleanse, please feel free to perform this cleanse as often as needed.

1. On a clear day, find a bright patch of sunlight to sit in, be it indoors or outdoors.

2. Sitting cross-legged, close your eyes and tilt your head toward the sun. Feel its energy and warmth, and take in its healing light.

3. Breathe in inner peace, your calming center, and hold on to it. You'll know once you're there.

4. Hold on to the feeling and the moment. Breathing deeply, count down from ten, then say these words:

My intent is pure;

My intent is clear.

Fire, water, air, and wind,

I ask you to fill me with positive energy.

Wind, air, water, and fire,

My intent is true.

Feel my positive energy;

Bless it back to me times three.

5. Once you have fed on positive energy and thoughts, it's time to begin your journey out of the shadows, uncovering the secrets and delights of the positivity witchery can bring.

Athame, Knife, Dagger, or Blade

An athame or a knife, dagger, or blade is used for rituals, ceremonies, pruning herbs, and more. An old kitchen knife will suffice. My athame is from Athens. It's an engraved dagger that I love, silver in coloring. Little touches like that can help personalize your altar and make you feel more connected to it.

Wand

A wand should definitely be part of your tool kit. You can use a traditional one made of wood, use a tree branch as a wand, or turn an elongated crystal into a wand.

Pendulum

A pendulum is a small weight suspended by a string or rope and is a tool utilized to gain information. To use it, simply ask and focus on a question and observe which direction the pendulum swings to obtain your answer. You can buy a pendulum, but making one is fairly easy. Simply find a strong string, chain, or cord about ten inches (25 cm) in length and add a small weight to it, such as a crystal pendant which is popular. Be sure to cleanse your pendulum (whether homemade or store bought) before using it. Finally, program your pendulum to show you "Yes" then ask it to show you "No." Follow this up by asking the pendulum "Yes/No" questions such as, "Is my name turmeric?" to program it.

Coarse Salt (or Sea Salt)

One of the most sacred minerals, salt represents protection as well as prosperity. Salt is often used in spellwork to create protective barriers (a circle of salt), cleansing, and banishing. Salt is also useful for drawing symbols for a spell. Use a thin layer of salt on a flat surface (such as a table or tray) and draw the symbol with your finger or wand.

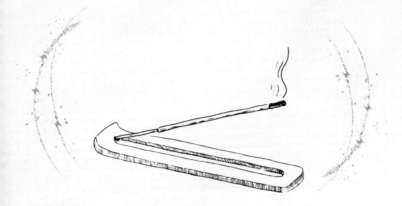

Incense

Incense is typically used at the beginning of a spell, but it can also be used for smudging small objects (like a small glass jar).

Witchcraft Procedures

In addition to the tools covered, there are a couple of common procedures that the following spells will require in this journal.

Anointing

There are several methods to bless or anoint an object. With all of the techniques below, be sure your intent is clear and that you're in a calm state of mind, as your energy is your most powerful tool. The most common methods to bless or anoint objects are:

★ Passing an object through smoke; typically incense or white sage is used for this process.

* Anointing the object with oil; sometimes this means drawing a symbol on the object (or person) with oil or rubbing the top of the object with oil, like a candle.

* Asking the moon to bless an object when it's a full moon; you can leave the object under direct moonlight until morning.

The Four Elements

The four elements (earth, air, water, and fire) are often used in spellwork. The materials typically used to represent the elements are the pentacle symbol and salt (earth), bells and incense (air), cauldron and chalice (water), and wand and candles (fire). Element representations, or tools, are often placed on altars and used for casting circles, spellwork, and for cleansing and consecrating rituals.

Moon Phases

Harnessing the power of a moon phase can strengthen spells and rituals. Channeling the moon's energy adds to your power. Working with nature is key, and moon phases are no different. Depending on the moon phase in which you perform a spell or ritual, your spellwork can be affected. On the following page are some things to keep in mind about the moon phases and their characteristics when performing magick and rituals:

New/Dark Moon

Because a new/dark moon represents a new beginning and fresh start, this is a perfect time period to start new rituals and practice spells to attract positivity and prosperity.

Waxing Moon (Waxing Gibbous, First Quarter, Waxing Crescent)

Because the moon grows during this phase, this is a period to continue to focus on positive intentions, creativity, and energy to bring good changes to your life that make you and your magick stronger.

Full Moon

This is when the moon is the strongest and most powerful and is and ideal phase to focus spells and rituals that need extra power and strength as well as a perfect phase to practice divination spells.

Waning Moon (Waning Gibbous, Last Quarter, Waning Crescent)

Because this phase is then the moon diminishes and gets ready for the next new moon, this is a retrospective period that challenges you to look inward and practice spells that remove unhealthy habits and negative energy in your life.

Healing
& Harmony
Spells

Before getting into other types of spells, such as spells for luck or love, it's best to first "cleanse your palate," so to speak. Spells work from the energy of our surroundings, as well as energy derived from the spellcaster. Make sure your aura and energy are as cleansed as possible by finding harmony within yourself first. That isn't to say that some of the spells in this section must be performed first or in a particular order; it is, however, suggested that you begin here, as these spells can assist in bringing inner peace. When doing spellwork, you want as much clarity as possible in your intentions and as much positive energy you can muster. May these spells help you along the way.

Goodnight, Sweet Dreams

Sometimes we can be plagued by nightmares. This spell can help keep your nights peaceful.

INGREDIENTS
1 teaspoon dried chamomile
1 teaspoon dried rosemary
1 bay leaf
3 cloves garlic
Handful of sea salt
5 drops lavender essential oil
3 drops jasmine essential oil
Glass bottle (or jar) with cork or lid
Long spoon
Metallic silver candle

INSTRUCTIONS

1. Add all the ingredients to the bottle (or jar). As you mix them together with the long spoon, meditate on your intention to eliminate bad dreams.

2. Light the candle. Speak the incantation as the flame burns. Cap the bottle with a cork or lid and use the candle wax to seal the top. Place the jar beside your bed for peaceful sleep.

INCANTATION

Blessed be,
Let this charm jar bring peace to me.
Let my sleep and my dreams go unmarred.
This I ask, free from harm.
So mote it be.

SPELL NOTES:

DATE: TIME:

MOON PHASE:

RESULTS/MODIFICATIONS:

What can you do to give yourself the best sleep possible?

_____

_____

_____

_____

_____

What dream in recent memory left you with the best feeling?

_____

_____

_____

_____

_____

Reflect on some of your most vivid dreams. What did you do, eat, or drink before bed?

_____

_____

_____

_____

_____

Spiritual Rejuvenation

Sometimes a spiritual weariness can come over us. You may feel fine, yet at the same time something isn't quite right. This means it is a good time for spiritual rejuvenation. The spell below combines a special tea with spiritual healing stones. The water acts as a conduit, and the stones as an anchor.

INGREDIENTS

1 quart (1 L) water
Heatproof pot
¼ cup (30 g) dried sweet birch bark
¼ cup (22 g) dried ginger
¼ cup (30 g) dried yarrow
Colander or cheesecloth
Mixing bowl
4 labradorite stones
1 purple amethyst quartz
2 lapis lazuli stones
2 white pillar candles
2 cups (680 g) Epsom salt

CUSTOMIZATION

For the amethyst quartz or lazuli stones, if you own a piece of jewelry with the stones in it (an amethyst ring, for example), this can be used in lieu of the stones as it connects the spell to you more intimately. Additionally, if you have a favorite T-shirt, this can be used to strain the special tea instead of the colander or cheesecloth.

INSTRUCTIONS

1. Pour the water into a heatproof pot. Add the sweet birch bark and ginger and bring to a boil. Reduce the heat to a low simmer and simmer for ten minutes.

2. Add the dried yarrow and continue to simmer for ten minutes longer.

3. Carefully strain the tea with your preferred item (colander, cheesecloth, or T-shirt) into the mixing bowl.

4. Once tea is prepared, place one labradorite stone in each corner of your tub (if your tub is round, just try to keep the stones equidistant). Place the purple amethyst at the head of the tub and the lapis lazuli on the right and left sides. Place the white pillar candles at the head of the tub on the right and left sides.

5. Fill the tub with water to the desired temperature, slowing mixing in the Epsom salt as you do. Then add the tea mixture.

6. Light the candles, turn off the lights, and then enter the bath. Take a moment of silence before saying the incantation.

INCANTATION

Renew and restore,

Restore and renew.

Goddess Idun, replenish my soul.

SPELL NOTES:

DATE: TIME:

MOON PHASE:

RESULTS/MODIFICATIONS:

What was your last mistake? How did you learn from it?

How can you positively disrupt your weekly routine?

What change has occurred in the last six months that you are
thankful for?

Emotional Cleansing Ritual

Sometimes it's hard to figure out how you feel about a person or situation since emotions can become murky. This ritual can help you clarify and streamline your feelings.

INGREDIENTS

Parchment paper
Red and blue markers
Salt (sea salt preferable, but any will do)
Burning bowl (or cauldron)
Van-Van Oil Blend (see page 15)
Blue candle
Wooden match

INSTRUCTIONS

I. During the day, preferably in a sunny spot, take your parchment paper and marker and write out words of how you feel (rage, sorrow, lost, etc.). There doesn't have to be a format to how you write on the paper—it can be akin to doodles with words. Once the paper is full of your emotions, tear the paper into large pieces.

2. Pour a little of the salt into the bottom of the burning bowl, which will help absorb negative energy.

3. With the Van-Van Oil Blend, anoint the blue candle, applying it with your fingers from the bottom of the candle upward to the wick. Light the candle with the wooden match.

4. Burn each piece of the paper, letting the fire consume it in the burning bowl. As it burns, say the incantation.

5. Bury the contents of the burning bowl. Place a few drops of the peace oil blend over the burial spot to complete the ritual.

INCANTATION

With fire and salt,
I purify my emotions, my spirit, myself.
As the fire burns, so does my pain.
Purifying fire and salt set me free.

SPELL NOTES:

DATE: TIME:

MOON PHASE:

RESULTS/MODIFICATIONS:

After you complete this ritual, take a moment outside in the fresh air, letting your feelings settle. Make a new list of words describing how you feel.

_____

_____

_____

_____

Create a list of positive words describing your emotions today.

_____

_____

_____

_____

What are three things about your emotions you value the most?

_____

_____

_____

_____

Bidding the Past Goodbye

A big part of the path to healing and finding harmony in your present is releasing the past. But for many, this can be hard to achieve seeing as the past can latch on to us with unforgiving jaws. Here's a tea spell bath to help you let the past go and find growth and peace. This ritual is performed during the last quarter of the moon. This is best performed outdoors once all the ingredients are ready.

INGREDIENTS

1 ounce (28 g) dried lavender
2 teaspoons dried passionflower
½ teaspoon dried ginger
1 teaspoon dried valerian root
Heatproof pot
1 quart (1 L) rainwater
Deep glass bowl
White candle (purity of intentions)
Blue candle (calmness and wisdom)
Red candle (passion for life)

CUSTOMIZATION

If rainwater is unavailable, purified water is a suitable substitute. If there is a specific person you wish to let go of, you may also tweak the incantation to speak their name aloud.

INSTRUCTIONS

1. Place the lavender, passionflower, ginger, and valerian root into the heatproof pot and add the rainwater. Bring to a boil, turn down the heat, and let simmer for fifteen minutes. Remove from the heat and let cool completely.

2. Pour the cooled tea into a deep, glass bowl. Light the candles in this order: white, blue, and then red. Focus on your inner light as you do so, and your desire for inner peace.

1. Use the tea to give yourself a bird bath (face, neck, hands, and arms), washing away the past as you say the incantation.

2. Once complete, sit and meditate, thinking of all the good tidings you want to bring your way in the near future.

INCANTATION

Heavy heart, weighted past,

I release you into the ether.

Weighted past, heavy heart,

I release you away from me.

I release you; I release myself.

I release myself.

I release myself.

SPELL NOTES:

DATE: TIME:

MOON PHASE:

RESULTS/MODIFICATIONS:

What are five things you like to do this month?

What is holding you back from doing something you want to do?

What are some things from your past you would like to say goodbye to?

Gratitude Spell

Every once in a while it's good to reflect on the positive things and energies in life and give thanks. Giving gratitude is a way to give back to the powers that be. Spellwork gives, and therefore, we should give back in return.

INGREDIENTS

2 ounces (60 ml) olive oil
1 sprig of fresh rosemary
Small bowl
White candle
Items to represent what you're thankful for
(something sentimental like a book or representative like a coin)

CUSTOMIZATION

You can use a sigil (an inscribed or painted symbol) to represent what you're thankful for.

INSTRUCTIONS

1. Combine the olive oil and rosemary in a small bowl. Anoint the candle with the mixture.

2. Light the candle, reflecting on each item you're presenting and what it means to you. Once each meaning is firm in your mind, speak aloud what you're thankful for.

3. Thank the elements for your blessings.

SPELL NOTES:

DATE: _____ **TIME:** _____

MOON PHASE: _____

RESULTS/MODIFICATIONS: _____

_____

_____

_____

_____

_____

_____

_____

_____

_____

_____

_____

_____

_____

_____

_____

_____

What people in your life are you grateful for?

_____

_____

_____

_____

_____

Can you name three things you're grateful for?

_____

_____

_____

_____

_____

What made you feel good about yourself this week and made you feel grateful?

_____

_____

_____

_____

_____

Clear Head

This spell makes use of a crystal grid, which is simply a pattern (a circle, square, spiral, or triangle) made of crystals and stones. A crystal grid will help supercharge the crystals and thus amplify the power of this spell. The center crystal is the focal point and should be larger than the other crystals you use. It's best to do this spell on a sunny day. If you have something personal to you like a necklace, ring, or feather place the item within the grid, connecting you more intimately to it. You can also use a wand, pendulum, or your hand to activate the grid.

INGREDIENTS

Crystal grid (optional)
Various quartz and crystal stones
A large clear crystal
Personal item (optional)
Wand (or pendulum)

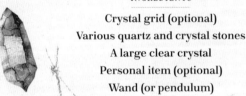

Crystal Grids

Crystal grids have many uses, such as cleansing or protecting a space, amplifying the power of crystals, and directing healing. The stones are set on a geometric pattern with the center stone being the largest. For placement of the crystals, follow your intuition. The patterns are meant to release absorbable energy, transforming your environment.

INSTRUCTIONS

I. If you have one, place a crystal grid on a table or the floor in a quiet space where there's sunlight. If you don't have a crystal grid, simply arrange the stones in a way that's pleasing to you with the large clear crystal as the focal point. Add your personal item if you wish.

2. Once the grid is complete, empty your mind. Try to conjure up the sound of white noise or rain; focus on it. Look at the grid and visualize a white light emanating from it. Close your eyes and hold this image in your mind.

3. Take your wand, pendulum, or hand and allow it to hover over the crystals slowly and in a pattern. Say the incantation in its entirety five times, your voice growing quieter as you do so.

INCANTATION

Clear crystal, I beseech you—
Offer my mind clarity.
Clear crystal, I beseech you—
Ease my troubled thoughts.
Clear crystal, I beseech you—
Purge my mind of darkness.
Clear crystal, I beseech you—
Give me peace of mind.

SPELL NOTES:

DATE: TIME:

MOON PHASE:

RESULTS/MODIFICATIONS:

Try this spell three times within a month. Immediately after each instance, write down the thoughts that come to mind.

What songs or types of music give you a sense of calm?

What helps you find inspiration?

Antidepression Spell Jar

In conjunction with therapy and journaling, an antidepression spell jar can be helpful in the journey to healing. It's especially good when you have a case of the blues.

INGREDIENTS

Glass jar
Coarse sea salt
Eggshells from three eggs
Orange zest from half an orange
7 drops orange essential oil
Rose petals from three roses
2 sprigs of fresh rosemary
3 drops rosemary essential oil

INSTRUCTIONS

1. Layer the ingredients into the jar as follows: coarse sea salt (½ inch, or 1.3 cm, high), eggshells, orange zest, orange essential oil, rose petals, rosemary, and rosemary essential oil.

2. Charge the jar by rotating it between your palms as you speak the incantation three times.

3. Place the jar on your nightstand. You can also take it with you and keep it close during the day.

CUSTOMIZATION

f you wish to give an extra boost to your jar, use white eggshells and lye them your favorite color first before adding them to the jar.

INCANTATION

With this jar,
I banish dark thoughts, feelings, and energy.
Bring calm to my mind and spirit.
With this jar,
I invite happiness and love of self
Into my days and nights.
Blessed be.

SPELL NOTES:

DATE: TIME:

MOON PHASE:

RESULTS/MODIFICATIONS:

The kind of person I am not is:

When was the last time I felt blue? Why?

What steps can I take to stop feeling blue?

Peaceful Home Ritual

Not all things need protection. Sometimes, what's needed is a cause for peace in your home. Maybe there is tension between family members, or you're bringing a lot of work home, or something else is bringing down the overall energy in your home. Use this ritual to promote peace and tranquility in your home space.

INGREDIENTS

Light purple, pink, or lavender candle
Small trinket representing each member of your household
(stones, pieces of cloth, etc.)
Van-Van Oil Blend (see page 15)
Pinch of dried lavender
Pinch of dried chamomile
Rose petals
Small amethyst
Lavender-colored pouch
(about 5 x 5 inches [12.5 x 12.5 cm]; sew one if you can't find one)

INSTRUCTIONS

1. Anoint the candle and the trinkets with the Van-Van Oil Blend. Hold the trinkets and other ingredients (lavender, chamomile, rose petals, and amethyst) individually, focusing on bringing peace into your home.

2. Place the trinkets and other ingredients in the pouch. Light the candle and sit in front of it while holding the pouch in your hands. Speak aloud the incantation.

3. Set the pouch next to the candle and allow the candle to burn down completely.

4. Hang the pouch in your home (wherever there is the most activity of its inhabitants). If tension seems to build, repeat the chant while envisioning peace and tranquility emanating from the pouch.

INCANTATION

Calm my home, oh blessed goddess.
Set stress free from my home and me;
Release all tension away,
Bringing calm, peace, and light.
Bless my home, powerful goddess,
Bring calm to my home.
Blessed be.

SPELL NOTES:

DATE: TIME:

MOON PHASE:

RESULTS/MODIFICATIONS:

What makes you feel at peace?

_____

_____

_____

_____

Are there any unresolved issues with people in your household? If so, what can you do to make amends?

_____

_____

_____

_____

What makes you feel safe at home?

_____

_____

_____

_____

Peace on the Go

Bringing peace into your life makes for more restful sleeping patterns, lower blood pressure, and a better overall disposition. Try this easy spell that's easy to take with you, spreading peace wherever you go.

INGREDIENTS

Pan
Rainwater (or distilled water)
Freshly cut parsley
3 drops Van-Van Oil Blend (see page 15)
Spray bottle

INSTRUCTIONS

I. Fill the pan with rainwater. Scatter the parsley cuttings on top of the water.

2. Swirl the parsley cuttings around as you speak the incantation three times.

3. Allow the pan to soak in a patch of moonlight all night, then place it in a patch of sunlight until the sun hits high noon.

4. Add the Van-Van Oil Blend to the spray bottle then pour the water into the bottle to fill it. Spray the water throughout the area in which you plan to bring peace, visualizing a calm environment as you do so.

CUSTOMIZATION

Add blue lace agate or black tourmaline to the mixture in the spray bottle to give this spell a calming boost.

INCANTATION

Cleansing water, restore peace.
Cleansing water, bring calm.
Cleansing water, create serenity.

SPELL NOTES:

DATE: TIME:

MOON PHASE:

RESULTS/MODIFICATIONS:

What is no longer serving you and making you feel ill at ease? What can you do to change it?

_____

_____

_____

_____

_____

What are the things that you truly need to feel peaceful?

_____

_____

_____

_____

What peaceful emotions do you want to begin feeling in the future?

_____

_____

_____

_____

_____

Creating a Blessed Charm

To convert an object into a charm, which can help enhance a spell, you first need to bless it as a call to action.

INGREDIENTS

2 black candles
3 white candles
Object to be blessed
Consecrated water in a glass dish (see page 11)

INSTRUCTIONS

I. In a room bathed in sunlight, create a pentagram on the floor (see following page). Place the black candles on the left and right edge of the pentagram, and the white candles in the three corners on the top and bottom of the pentagram.

2. Place your object to be blessed in the glass dish with consecrated water in the middle of the pentagram. Facing the pentagram, speak the incantation.

INCANTATION

With the power of the sun,
I ask that you bless and imbue this [NAME OF OBJECT]
with your power.
Protect it from darkness and harm.
Blessed be.

Pentagram

A pentagram can be made out of many objects or items, including salt, chalk, wood gathered in a natural setting (such as the beach, forest, desert, park, etc.), stones, crystals, or if you prefer something more permanent like paint.

SPELL NOTES:

DATE: TIME:

MOON PHASE:

RESULTS/MODIFICATIONS:

What charm did you chose? Why?

_____

_____

_____

_____

What arc your hopes as you begin this journal?

_____

_____

_____

_____

What do you think you will encounter on your journey?

_____

_____

_____

_____

Heal Thy Emotions Spell Jar

While there are many spells for healing, this one targets emotional pain. Healing of this nature takes time, but this spell jar can help expedite the process.

INGREDIENTS

2 ounces (60 g) rock salt
Small glass jar
Blue lace agate
Handful of ivy
1 sprig of fresh peppermint leaves
7 drops rosemary essential oil

INSTRUCTIONS

I. Pour the rock salt into the bottom of the jar to act as a cleansing agent. Place the blue lace agate on top. Layer on the ivy and peppermint leaves. Finally, drizzle the rosemary essential oil on the top.

2. Placing both hands over the jar, speak the incantation three times.

3. Before screwing on the lid, charge the jar by allowing it to bathe in sunlight for an hour.

4. Keep the jar close to you. Use it as a focal point for meditation or while taking a bath in a quiet, peaceful environment.

CUSTOMIZATION

Instead of, or in addition to the rock salt, you can also add pink Himalayan salt to the jar. This salt is not only nice to look at, but it can also increase the cleansing and purification properties of the spell.

INCANTATION

With these words,
I charge this jar
To bring healing and peace.

SPELL NOTES:

DATE: TIME:

MOON PHASE:

RESULTS/MODIFICATIONS:

How can you better love yourself?

What is a word that best describes your emotions today (happy, fun, vibrant, etc.) and why?

How can you best stay present in your emotions?

Power
Spells

This section is about reclaiming your power in some shape or form. Power means taking control of your well-being and cleansing it of inner negativity. These spells will help build your courage and trust in yourself and your intuition. Personal power is about self-defining your nature and setting limits while having freedom. Unlocking your personal power will allow you to experience a new and true side of yourself.

As without, so shall be within.

Negating Negativity Spell

This is an easy spell to do after an evening shower. It will release any accrued negative energy from the day and help attract positivity and prosperity into your life.

INGREDIENTS

Pitcher
8 teaspoons (18 g) ground cinnamon
8 teaspoons (48 g) coarse salt
2 quarts (2 L) water

INSTRUCTIONS

1. In a pitcher, combine the cinnamon, salt, and water as you speak the incantation. Set aside in your bathroom. Shower normally.

2. Once finished showering, pour the mixture onto your body from the neck down, cleansing the negativity from you.

Herbal Teas

Herbal teas can help promote health of the body and mind, and some are meant to uplift the soul. Rosemary tea is said to aid in clearing negative thoughts and general clutter, offering clarity. Thyme tea has been consumed for centuries to promote creativity and passion for writing as well as help with speaking and communication.

INCANTATION

With the protection of cinnamon and salt
And the cleansing purity of water,
Negative forces, I banish thee away from me.
I release you; you may not stay.
Negative energy, be on your way.
So mote it be.

SPELL NOTES:

DATE: _____ TIME: _____

MOON PHASE: _____

RESULTS/MODIFICATIONS: _____

_____

_____

_____

_____

_____

_____

_____

_____

_____

_____

_____

_____

_____

What brought on negativity this day? How can you avoid it tomorrow?

_____

_____

_____

_____

What are some beautiful moments you've experienced this week that counter any negativity?

_____

_____

_____

_____

What can you do differently tomorrow to avoid being negative?

_____

_____

_____

_____

Courage Jar

Sometimes courage can be hard to come by in day-to-day life. Maybe you need the courage to speak up for yourself, take an important step in life, or simply pursue your own happiness. The courage jar is best kept in a place where you frequent most, such as a nightstand in your bedroom or an office desk.

INGREDIENTS

Tiger's eye
Anointing oil blend (see page 17)
Small glass jar
Black tea leaves
2 dried bay leaves
1 cinnamon stick

INSTRUCTIONS

1. First anoint the tiger's eye with the anointing oil blend. Then place it at the bottom of the jar, followed by the black tea leaves, the bay leaves (break into pieces, if necessary), and the cinnamon stick.

2. Focus on your intent for courage in your everyday life as you recite the incantation.

INCANTATION

Oh, blessed goddess, enchant this jar.
Let this represent the strength I have inside of me,
And allow it to grow.
Let this charm bring out my courage.
Grant me the power to speak and to act.

SPELL NOTES:

DATE: TIME:

MOON PHASE:

RESULTS/MODIFICATIONS:

What things (or people) cause you to be fearful? What power do they have over you?

What are three things you can do to be more courageous this week?

What are three steps you can take to become stronger?

Courage Charm

Much like the courage jar (see page 66), this charm can promote strength to speak your truth and act. This charm is portable, and you can carry it with you everywhere, keeping courage close by your side.

INGREDIENTS

5 drops orange essential oil
2 tablespoons (30 ml) of carrier oil of choice (see page 14)
Several black peppercorns
Pinch of dried basil
Pinch of dried thyme
Orange sachet
Red ribbon or thread

CUSTOMIZATION

To help personalize your jar, place something symbolic within it that represents courage but that also has a direct connection. Examples include charms such as lions, dragons, eagles, arrows, anchors, etc.

INSTRUCTIONS

I. Blend the orange essential and carrier oils and sprinkle over the peppercorns, basil, and thyme. Put the herbs and peppercorn into the sachet, speaking the incantation on the following page.

2. Tie the bag with the red ribbon or thread. Keep it close to you always—in your bag, purse, or pocket. Keep it underneath your pillow as you sleep.

3. On the next full moon, replace the herbs and oil, speaking the incantation again.

4. Once you feel the purpose has been served, untie the knot of the ribbon or thread and bury the satchel.

INCANTATION

Blessed goddess, grant me the strength
of a bear and the fearlessness of a lion.
Allow me bravery and truth.
Grant me courage for today and tomorrow.
Oh goddess, bless me with the strength and fearlessness
To do what I must.
Blessed be.

SPELL NOTES:

DATE: .... TIME: ....

MOON PHASE: ....

RESULTS/MODIFICATIONS: ....

What does courage mean to you? How has it impacted your life?

What's the most courageous thing you've ever done?

Who is the most courageous person you know? Why?

Anger Release Ritual

So many of us can be consumed by anger at a situation or a person. Anger is a natural part of life. However, it's when you cannot release anger that it becomes problematic. This spell is meant to give you a boost in letting the anger go and moving on. This ritual is best done in the morning when you wake up.

INGREDIENTS

Smudge stick
Burning bowl (or cauldron)
Wood matches
Red candle
2 sheets of paper
Pen
White candle
Green sachet

INSTRUCTIONS

I. Find a quiet space, light the smudge stick, and cleanse the room. Once complete, put out the smoldering smudge stick by dabbing the burning end into the burning bowl. Stand and close your eyes, envisioning a white light encircling you, protecting you.

2. As you face each of the four cardinal points, recite the incantation.

3. Face east and call upon the element of air, beseeching it to help you express your rage.

4. Face south and call upon the element of fire to help incinerate any trauma of the past that has brought forth your rage.

5. Face west and call upon the element of water to help unblock your emotions, allowing them to flow freely and restore your true self.

6. Face the north and call upon the element of earth to keep you grounded

7. Close your eyes and once again envision the white light encircling you, giving protection.

8. Light the red candle, then write about the anger that you cannot release on one piece of paper. Fold the paper twice and hold it tightly as you speak aloud your trauma and anger. Shout if you must, sending the energy into the flame of the red candle. Once released, quickly burn the paper and put it into the burning bowl.

9. Light the white candle. Write about the things that bring you peace on the second piece of paper and the good things that you want to attract to you. Fold the paper and place it into the sachet.

10. Scatter the ashes from the burning bowl into the wind away from you, thanking the four elements and the higher powers for assisting you.

11. Place the sachet in the pillowcase that you place your head on; this will promote positive energy and thoughts.

INCANTATION

I call upon the air to help me speak my rage aloud.
I call upon the fire to burn away the ills that have plagued my thoughts.
I call upon the water to cleanse me and bring me back to my true form.
I call upon the earth to ground me and give me footing.

SPELL NOTES:

DATE: TIME:

MOON PHASE:

RESULTS/MODIFICATIONS:

Write down any negativity, anger, or destructive feelings, releasing them onto the page. How can you change them into positive feelings?

Think about the most recent thing that made you angry. How can you respond differently? Would that change the outcome of your feelings?

How does your anger empower you?

Sever All Ties

While most commonly used for exes, this spell can also be utilized for a former friend or foe. Severing all ties is something that should be done only when you're certain you want nothing to do with the person. As this is a huge step, it's imperative to proceed with certainty that you're ready.

INGREDIENTS

Scissors

Van-Van Oil Blend (see page 15)

A photograph of you and a photograph
of the person you want to sever ties with (or two tarot cards that are
representative of you and your ex)

A piece of silver ribbon (about 6 inches, or 15 cm)

INSTRUCTIONS

1. Anoint your scissors with the Van-Van Oil Blend. Set aside.

2. On your altar (or a cleansed table), place the two photographs down and side by side. Lay the ribbon horizontally between the two photos, connecting them.

3. Place your index and forefinger from both hands on the ribbon, one for each picture. Close your eyes and envision a white room where the person is standing before you. Interact with them in this space how you like. The visualization is for the purpose of bringing closure. You can scream, argue, kiss, whatever you need to do in the comfort of this visualized space.

4. Once you have said/done what you need, tell them goodbye, and then open your eyes. Speak the incantation two times. On the third time of speaking the incantation, take the anointed scissors and cut the ribbon in half to complete the spell.

CUSTOMIZATION

The ribbon you used can be from a fabric that has connection to you and the person, such as from a shirt or laces from a pair of shoes.

INCANTATION

That which blocks me from moving forward
Keeps me from receiving what I deserve,
With the power of three times three,
I release these ties that have bound me,
Moving forward with freedom and light in my heart.
So mote it be.

SPELL NOTES:

DATE: TIME:

MOON PHASE:

RESULTS/MODIFICATIONS:

What, specifically, do you need to heal by removing this person from your life?

_____

_____

_____

_____

What has this person taught you?

_____

_____

_____

_____

What have you learned from the time shared with this person?

_____

_____

_____

_____

_____

Free from the Past Spell

If growth and happiness are what you seek, this spell will help you reveal and release the mental and emotional ties that have been holding you back. This spell is best performed during daylight.

INGREDIENTS

White candle
Blue candle
Red candle
Deep glass bowl
Rainwater (or purified water)
1 bunch of fresh basil

INSTRUCTIONS

I. Choose your environment—alone outdoors or a quiet space indoors with sunlight access (window, skylight, etc.). Arrange the candles from left to right: white, blue, and red. Light them in order and speak the following incantation:

INCANTATION

White for pure, divine light and purity of my intentions.

Blue for the wisdom of the universe and to bring calm.

Red for my passion of life.

2. Fill the glass bowl with rainwater and place the basil in it, swirling it around. Wash your face and neck with the water. Focus on moving forward into your future, then speak the following incantation.

INCANTATION

Release the ties that bind me to my past.

Cut the cords and set me free.

To yesterday, I bid goodbye.

3. Blow out the candles. Sit and meditate on both the present and the future you want for yourself.

SPELL NOTES:

DATE: TIME:

MOON PHASE:

RESULTS/MODIFICATIONS:

How can you give yourself more support?

_____

_____

_____

_____

What has been overwhelming you lately?

_____

_____

_____

_____

What from your past has been holding you back?

_____

_____

_____

_____

_____

Empower Thyself

If you find your self-esteem to be on the low side, this spell will help give it a boost.

INGREDIENTS

3 drops orange essential oil

2 tablespoons (30 ml) of carrier oil of choice (see page 14)

½ teaspoon yarrow

Small jar

Red candle

Rose quartz

Citrine

Amethyst

Yarrow herb has a multitude of uses and medicinal properties. Its origin goes back to ancient Rome when soldiers used the plant to staunch wounds. Other uses include soothing stings, bites, cuts, and alleviating fever in tea form.

INSTRUCTIONS

1. Blend the orange essential and carrier oils and combine them with the yarrow in a small jar. Anoint the candle with the mixture.

2. Light the candle and then focus on the flame as you think about your inner energy.

3. One by one, take each crystal and pass it through the flame, chanting the incantation in full for each one.

4. Do this daily for seven days. After the seventh day, whenever you feel low, visualize the candle in your mind's eye and repeat the incantation internally.

INCANTATION

I am good.

I am enough.

I am strength.

I am power.

SPELL NOTES:

DATE: _____   TIME: _____

MOON PHASE: _____

RESULTS/MODIFICATIONS: _____

_____

_____

_____

_____

_____

_____

_____

_____

_____

_____

_____

_____

_____

Where does your strength come from?

What areas need more powers in your life?

What would help you feel more empowered? How can you go about achieving it?

Protection Spells

When we think of protection spells, our personal spaces typically come to mind. This section will explore protection from our emotions, since sometimes we can be our own greatest saboteurs while other times we need protection from the emotions of others. Some of us are empathic, and we take on the negative energy of others and allow it to weigh us down. There are many types of protection. Through spells and journaling, it's my hope that you can figure out the type of protection that will best serve you going forward.

Protection Charm Jar from the Evil Eye

The evil eye is a curse that can cause a plethora of unsavory outcomes, from bad luck to ailments. It's usually a manifestation of a person wishing you ill due to jealousy, hatred, or greed. It's hard to know how or when an evil eye may strike, which is why it's a good idea to carry a protection talisman. One of the most common forms is a blue glass bead that looks like an eye, called a nazar. While a talisman is helpful, this spell also offers a customization to specifically protect you or a loved one. It must be stated: To avoid the draw of the evil eye, it would behoove you not to brag and to avoid drawing ire from others.

The Evil Eye

The belief in the curse of the evil eye spans cultures, generations, and millennia. Nearly every culture has its own variation of the evil eye legend, such as the petrifying gaze of the Gorgons in Greek mythology. Despite its pagan connotations, references to the evil eye can even be found in religious texts, from the Bible to the Qur'an. The first recorded mention of the evil eye is believed to be from 5,000 years ago on clay tablets in cuneiform writing by the Mesopotamians.

INGREDIENTS

NOTE: *The size of your jar will dictate how much of the ingredients to use. Should you decide to use a larger vessel, adjust your ingredients accordingly.*

White candle
Small piece of amber (or citrine)
3 drops of protection oil blend (see page 16)
1 part coarse sea salt
Small glass jar with a cork (1½ to 2 inches, or 3.8 to 5 cm, tall)
1 part dried sage
1 part dried lavender
2 sandalwood chips
1 part dried frankincense

INSTRUCTIONS

I. Anoint the white candle and piece of amber (or citrine) with the protection oil blend. Add a bit of salt to the bottom of the glass jar, then add the piece of amber. Layer the sage, lavender, sandalwood, and frankincense over it. Cork the vessel.

2. Light the candle. Activate the charm jar with the incantation below as the candle burns.

3. Continue the chant until the wax pools on the surface of the candle, then bind the jar by allowing the wax to drip over the top of the bottle (the sides of the opening and the top of the cork) as you speak the incantation. Let it cool.

4. Your charm is ready to be carried around with you for protection. Also place it on your nightstand or near your bed as you sleep.

INCANTATION

Blessed charm,

Protect me from evil glares.

Blessed charm,

Protect me from evil thoughts.

Blessed charm,

Please keep me safe.

Blessed charm,

Bless me.

SPELL NOTES:

DATE: TIME:

MOON PHASE:

RESULTS/MODIFICATIONS:

What have you been envious of recently? Why?

How can you be less envious and more grateful for what you have?

What is a strength of yours that can be used to help someone or give
back to the world?

Leave Me Alone Spell

Every once in a while a nuisance can appear in our lives, causing distractions—or worse, chaos. This simple and harmless spell will help restore the peace that you desire.

INGREDIENTS

1 garlic clove
Small knife
Sheet of paper
Blue pen

INSTRUCTIONS

I. Cut the clove of garlic in half with the knife. Rub the pieces all over the sheet of paper. The garlic acts as a banishing charger.

2. Write the full name of the person who you want to leave you alone, then draw a circle around it. Fold the sheet of paper up as tightly and small as you can.

3. Place the folded paper in the very back of your freezer as you speak the incantation.

INCANTATION

Leave me alone,

Away with you.

Let this spell grant me peace,

And solitude.

Away and leave.

So mote it be.

SPELL NOTES:

DATE: TIME:

MOON PHASE:

RESULTS/MODIFICATIONS:

Take ten minutes to write the names of the people you are grateful to have in your life.

_____

_____

_____

_____

Which people in your life bring you the most joy? Have you let them know?

_____

_____

_____

_____

What actions of yours may annoy others?

_____

_____

_____

_____

Protection Ritual (Bath)

There are many protection spells used for spaces, as barriers, as charms, and more. This is a spell that you can literally cover yourself in and wear. The ritual is meant to last for twenty-four to forty-eight hours and offers additional protection.

INGREDIENTS

Handful of coarse salt
1 bunch of fresh basil
1 bunch of fresh lavender (or 1 tablespoon of dry lavender)
1 sprig of fresh mint
2 sprigs of fresh rosemary
Bowl

INSTRUCTIONS

1. Run a hot (but not too hot) bath, putting in the salt and herbs under the running water. As the water runs, speak the incantation, gently mixing the herbs and salt. When the water level is to your liking, allow the bath to steep for a few minutes.

2. Soak in the bath, visualizing a protective energy emanating from the water and covering you.

3. When you're done with the bath, scoop a bit of the water and herbs into the bowl and toss it outside, completing the ritual.

CUSTOMIZATION

If you have a personal crystal (e.g., obsidian, amethyst, smoky quartz) that you keep close to you or as a piece of jewelry, add it to your bath (or wear the item) during the soak.

INCANTATION

Enchanted waters,
Bring protection when you wash over me.
Bless me and keep me from harm.

SPELL NOTES:

DATE: TIME:

MOON PHASE:

RESULTS/MODIFICATIONS:

Who makes you feel protected? Why?

What makes you feel powerful?

What makes you feel in control?

House Protection Ritual

As you know, stones and crystals hold powers. By using a special combination of them, you can perform a simple, noninvasive ritual to help protect your home that utilizes a special placement of the stones as well as your intent.

INGREDIENTS

Smudge stick
Burning bowl (or cauldron)
1 amethyst
1 black tourmaline
1 citrine
1 rose quartz
1 smoky quartz
1 obsidian

INSTRUCTIONS

1. To begin, smudge your home with the smudge stick, going over every floor and every room. Once complete, put out the smoldering smudge stick by dabbing the burning end into the burning bowl.

2. Hold all six stones in your palms, focusing on your intent for protection. Visualize the energy coming from them, charging them.

3. Place the amethyst in a safe place in your living room to help define boundaries while maintaining control.

4. Place the black tourmaline at your threshold, marking a clear division between your home and the outside world.

5. Place the citrine in the back left side of the home to attract happiness and health.

6. Place the rose quartz in the center of the home—the heart—to nurture a peaceful and harmonious environment.

7. Place the smoky quartz on a windowsill or in the main bedroom, directing negative energy away and offering a veil of protection.

8. Finally, place the obsidian in an entryway to cleanse and clear negative energy before it can enter.

SPELL NOTES:

DATE: TIME:

MOON PHASE:

RESULTS/MODIFICATIONS:

What feelings does your home evoke?

What can you do to make your home feel more comfortable?

What kind of energy do you feel in your home?

Threshold Protection Spell

It's important to protect what comes into your home from bringing in negative energy, from people to packages. Negative energy can travel and live on inanimate objects. Therefore, a spell of protection for your threshold can help curb negativity from entering your space. Smudging helps promote and invite positive energy into your home. Don't forget the other entryways into your home (back doors, porch doors, etc.). This spell is best to begin on the night of a full moon. Sprinkling this spell onto windowsills is also helpful.

INGREDIENTS

Smudge stick
Black candle
Burning bowl (or cauldron)
Handful of coarse sea salt
3 whole garlic cloves
Handful of fresh rosemary
Mixing bowl

CUSTOMIZATION

The garlic can be smashed, sliced, charred, or baked. Any of these measures will help bring out the essence from the garlic cloves. Follow your intuition.

INSTRUCTIONS

I. This spell works best if you begin with a clean slate, so first cleanse your entryways with a smudging. Light the smudge stick with the candle to strengthen the cleanse. Once complete, put out the smoldering smudge stick by dabbing the burning end into the burning bowl.

2. Stir together the sea salt, garlic, and rosemary in the mixing bowl. Leave the mixing bowl on a windowsill to be charged by the moonlight.

3. On the following morning, take the mixing bowl and spread the ingredients outside your front door. The bigger the entryway, or the more entryways you have, the more mixture you should use.

SPELL NOTES:

DATE: _____   **TIME:** _____

MOON PHASE: _____

RESULTS/MODIFICATIONS:

_____

_____

_____

_____

_____

_____

_____

_____

_____

_____

_____

_____

_____

_____

_____

_____

What actions can you take to keep your space peaceful?

How do you recharge your space?

What can you do today in your space that you couldn't do a year ago?

Eliminating Negative Energy Ritual

Negativity can manifest itself in many different ways. It can be brought on by thoughts or by the energy around us. Environments, just like people, can give off negative energy. Negative energy can also come from bad experiences or past traumas. Many people engage in smudging a space, like a home, to eliminate negativity. This ritual is also good for cleansing used objects.

INGREDIENTS

Smudge stick
Burning bowl (or cauldron)
Wooden matches

INSTRUCTIONS

1. Circle the smudge stick around the burning bowl, speaking the incantation to activate it.

2. With a wooden match, light the smudge stick. Blow it out quickly once it catches fire, allowing the leaves to slowly smolder and release a heavy smoke.

3. Speak the incantation once more as you wave the smudge stick around the object, or room, in a clockwise motion, allowing the smoke to linger and hang in the air. Be thorough with the smoke "coating." Allow the ash to fall into the burning bowl when necessary.

4. Once complete, put out the smoldering smudge stick by dabbing the burning end into the burning bowl.

INCANTATION

I release all negativity from me and this space/object.

Released and banished, leave this place.

Negative energy, this is my command.

So mote it be.

SPELL NOTES:

DATE: TIME:

MOON PHASE:

RESULTS/MODIFICATIONS:

After the spell is complete, sit in the room alone (or sit in a quiet room with the object) and try to pick up on the current energy. Write what you've discovered and how it makes you feel.

_____

_____

_____

_____

What helps you feel more grounded and present and less negative?

_____

_____

_____

_____

_____

What's a goal you need to accomplish to bring about positivity or eliminate negativity?

_____

_____

_____

_____

_____

The Top Five Crystals for Emotional Well-Being

AGATE helps neutralize negativity and bitterness while helping you overcome emotional trauma. It works best if kept close to your heart.

RED CALCITE can bring understanding, uplift your emotions, and alleviate fear. Calcite comes in several colors, and all of them promote some variant of emotional balance.

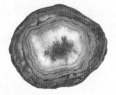

CARNELIAN removes emotional negativity in the wearer and also in those in close proximity. It promotes a zest for life and is best worn as a pendant.

AZURITE brings light to your emotions as it eases away stress and grief. It removes emotional blocks and has the power to transform your fears and phobias.

LARIMAR is a powerful healing crystal that is said to bring calm, peace, and emotional equilibrium. It's most potent if positioned over your heart, third eye, or solar plexus.

Protection Jar

Spells cast in jars are typically easy to make, but even better is that they're portable. You can put them in your purse, pocket, or bag, or if it's small enough, even wear it on a necklace or bracelet as a charm. Feel free to use a jar of any size you prefer.

INGREDIENTS

Glass jar with cork

Frankincense or sage incense

Burning bowl (or cauldron)

3 ounces (85 g) sea salt

5 drops of essence of lavender

Small bowl

1 bay leaf

Amethyst crystals (several small ones are easier for small bottles; one larger crystal for a larger bottle is sufficient)

2 ounces (60 g) dried calamine flowers

2 sprigs of fresh rosemary

Black candle

INSTRUCTIONS

I. First cleanse the jar with the incense. Get a good smoke going, then swirl the incense stick around the jar, allowing the smoke to fill it. Focus on your intent for protection during this time. Once complete, think about how you want to be protected for a moment. Put out the smoldering end by dabbing the burning end into the burning bowl.

2. Combine the sea salt and essence of lavender in a small bowl, then add the mixture to the jar about a third of the way full. Add the bay leaf (fold it to fit the jar if necessary), amethyst crystals, calamine flowers, and finally the rosemary. Cork the jar.

3. Light the candle, once again focusing on your intent, then allow the wax to drip all over the top of the cork and the sides, to seal the jar.

SPELL NOTES:

DATE: TIME:

MOON PHASE:

RESULTS/MODIFICATIONS:

What makes you feel safe? Where is your safe space?

Is there anything you feel you need protection from? What is it?

What can you do to feel protected and empowered?

Peace, Harmony, and Protection Ritual

It's always helpful to have a bit of peace and harmony accompany a protection ritual. Tranquility is good for the mind and the soul.

INGREDIENTS

1 part dried lavender
1 part dried betony
Mortar and pestle

INSTRUCTIONS

1. Blend the lavender and betony well with the mortar and pestle.

2. Charge the herb mixture by placing it in direct sunlight for one hour.

3. Sprinkle a small amount of the mixture across your doorsteps. As you do so, imagine a peaceful barrier of light while speaking the incantation.

INCANTATION

Let this doorstep be guarded by a shield,

Forged in magick and light.

Guard this home by day and by night.

Bad or negative energies dare not cross.

Only peace, harmony, and protection can pierce this seal.

SPELL NOTES:

DATE: _____ TIME: _____

MOON PHASE: _____

RESULTS/MODIFICATIONS:

_____

_____

_____

_____

_____

_____

_____

_____

_____

_____

_____

_____

_____

_____

_____

What was your journey of discovery to magick?

How have you felt harmony in your life?

What can you do to make the different parts of your life more harmonious with each other?

Luck &
Prosperity
Spells

Some people swear by good luck charms like a rabbit's foot, horseshoe, lucky coin, or a lucky sweater. Others make their own luck. Having a positive outlook and mindset can help manifest the power of luck and prosperity. What better way to bring prosperity to yourself and your home than with a little magick with the spells in this part!

New Beginnings

Sometimes we need to usher new beginnings into our lives. Fresh starts are often desired after reaching a milestone in life, such as a particular birthday or a change in relationship status. Having a blessing or spell for a fresh start can help mark the transition into something new.

INGREDIENTS

Black candle
Blue pen
Sheet of paper
Burning bowl (or cauldron)
Green candle
Wooden matches (preferable)

INSTRUCTIONS

1. On the day of a new moon in a calm environment (it can be indoors or outside), light the black candle.

2. With the pen and paper, write a list of your missteps, bad situations, failed relationships, and insecurities. Stick the corner into the flame and place it into the burning bowl. As it burns, say this incantation:

INCANTATION

Out with the old, away from me.
Your influences are finished.
The past is done, burnt to ash.
I banish thee. I banish thee. I banish thee.

3. Light the green candle, scatter the ashes into the air, and then chant this incantation:

INCANTATION

I beseech the energy of the universe
To bless me with a new path,
Bringing me change.
In with the new and out with the old.

SPELL NOTES:

DATE: TIME:

MOON PHASE:

RESULTS/MODIFICATIONS:

Are you able to set boundaries? How can you be more disciplined with that?

_____

_____

_____

_____

_____

What's an action plan you can make for tomorrow?

_____

_____

_____

_____

What's an important change you want in your life right now?

_____

_____

_____

_____

Prosperous Home

Everyone can use a little prosperity in life. Whether you wish to be prosperous emotionally, financially, or spiritually, this spell is for you. When the outside world takes its toll, we at least can have the respite of being in our own home, which is the foundation of our lives and should provide stability. May this spell bring good fortune, wealth, and luck.

INGREDIENTS

Your doormat (indoors or outdoors)
2 tablespoons dried basil
2 ounces (60 g) sandalwood chips
2 ounces (60 g) dried patchouli
1 silver coin

INSTRUCTIONS

1. Lift your doormat and sprinkle the basil, sandalwood, and patchouli under your doormat. In the center, place the silver coin. Replace the doormat.

2. Stand on the doormat facing north and speak the incantation three times.

INCANTATION

Let this mat welcome good fortune into my home.

Allow prosperity to cross my threshold.

Good fortune, luck, and success are welcome.

Positive energy is welcome.

SPELL NOTES:

DATE: **TIME:**

MOON PHASE:

RESULTS/MODIFICATIONS:

Do you feel prosperous? If yes, in what facets of your life? If no, why?

When it comes to prosperity of time, how is your time best spent?

What is one thing you can become better at that will allow you to be more prosperous?

𝕳𝖆𝖕𝖕𝖞 𝖁𝖎𝖇𝖊𝖘 𝕽𝖎𝖙𝖚𝖆𝖑

If you'd like to bring positive vibes and light into your life, try this ritual. It can uplift your energy and lighten your aura. Choose a flowering plant that's visually appealing to you and, if you can, one that's your favorite color (an orchid plant is a good go-to choice).

INGREDIENTS

Black pen
Sheet of paper
Yellow candle
Van-Van Oil Blend (see page 15)
Burning bowl (or cauldron)
5 drops lilac flower essence
Flowering plant of choice
Purified water

INSTRUCTIONS

1. Think carefully about the things that are making you unhappy. Think of words that describe your discontent. Write them out with the black pen on the sheet of paper.

2. Anoint the candle with the Van-Van Oil Blend. After lighting it, put the edge of the paper into the flame. Once it begins to burn, place it into the burning bowl, allowing it to burn completely to ash. As this takes place, visualize your problems evaporating, incinerated by the flame.

3. Gently rub a bit of the lilac flower essence onto the leaves and petals of the plant. Pour a little purified water into the burning bowl with the ashes. Pour the ash water onto the plant, representing you nourishing your happiness. Focus on positive energy and happiness, then blow out the candle.

CUSTOMIZATION

If you have green jasper, place it halfway into the soil after you pour the water and ash mixture to give the smell an extra boost.

SPELL NOTES:

DATE: TIME:

MOON PHASE:

RESULTS/MODIFICATIONS:

Do you feel happy? If no, why? If yes, to what do you attribute it?

Do you feel you bring happiness to others?

How do you define your happiness?

Positive Manifestation Spell

A wish is merely putting positive thoughts into the universe, attempting to draw what you desire to you. Maybe it's a dream job, or a great love, or money. With the power of positive intentions, this spell can help clarify what you desire and bring it to you.

INGREDIENTS

Metallic gold candle
Blue pen
Sheet of paper

INSTRUCTIONS

I. In a quiet space, light the candle. Close your eyes and for the next ten minutes think about specifically what you want—the job you want, the type of partner you want, the home you want, and so on. Keep your intent and desires strong but pure.

2. Write descriptors of the thing you desire on the paper. Feel free to use both sides. The words and phrase can be written randomly, but make sure you take up space on the page.

3. When you're finished, fold the paper into eighths. Hold it over the heat of the flame, but not in the flame (you don't want to burn the paper) and speak the incantation. Blow out the candle, then place the folded paper inside your pillowcase.

INCANTATION

Let this paper represent my deepest desires.

With my intent pure and clear,

And no harm to come to others,

I ask the universe to bring these to me.

SPELL NOTES:

DATE: TIME:

MOON PHASE:

RESULTS/MODIFICATIONS:

What new positive opportunities have come out of the challenges you've faced?

_____

_____

_____

_____

In what ways can you step outside of your comfort zone and be more positive?

_____

_____

_____

_____

How can you feel more connected to the universe to bring about positivity?

_____

_____

_____

_____

Money Jar

Wealth, prosperity, fortune. Who doesn't enjoy a good luck charm for money? This jar will work as an attractor to extra coins and monetary success.

INGREDIENTS

Paper
Green pen
Small glass jar
1 bay leaf
1 ounce (30 g) dried patchouli
8 coins (preferably silver)
1 teaspoon dried basil
Citrine

INSTRUCTIONS

1. With the paper and pen, write down your intent—what you need the money for, how much, where it should come from (a work bonus, the lottery, selling a product, etc.). Be as clear as possible. Fold it up tightly.

2. In the glass jar, add the bay leaf, patchouli, coins, basil, folded paper, and top it with the citrine. Screw on the top and keep it sealed until the jar brings about the desired wish.

CUSTOMIZATION

Instead of a piece of paper, you can use a deposit slip, a one-dollar bill, or something else that represents money.

SPELL NOTES:

DATE: TIME:

MOON PHASE:

RESULTS/MODIFICATIONS:

What is your relationship with money now? What do you want it to be?

_____

_____

_____

_____

What is the most valuable currency to you?

_____

_____

_____

_____

If you ran out of money tomorrow, what would you do?

_____

_____

_____

_____

_____

Cinnamon Money Spell

Cinnamon has many uses in spellwork. One of the most common uses is for prosperity and money. This spell will help attract both to you and your household.

INGREDIENTS

3 cinnamon sticks
Burning bowl (or cauldron)

INSTRUCTIONS

I. On the night of a crescent moon, go outside into the moonlight with your materials. Circle the cinnamon sticks around the burning bowl, speaking the incantation three times.

2. Light the cinnamon sticks (like incense). Put out the smoldering end by dabbing the burning end into the burning bowl. Capture some of the ash in the burning bowl.

3. Sprinkle the ashes at your doorstep.

A versatile spice, cinnamon is considered one of the most ancient spices. True cinnamon is harvested from the inner bark of large evergreen trees of the genus Cinnamomum. Most cinnamon products are from Cassia, a related species. The difference in color and thickness of their sticks is important; true cinnamon is thinner and lighter in color and has a fainter scent. Cassia is more commonly sold in stores than true cinnamon.

INCANTATION

With the power of three times three,
And by the light of this crescent moon,
Bring luck and prosperity to my home and to me.

SPELL NOTES:

DATE: TIME:

MOON PHASE:

RESULTS/MODIFICATIONS:

What is one thing you could do to improve your financial life?

What do you want your financial future to look like?

How does money bring you joy?

Receive Money Spell

This spell is a bit more direct when it comes to money (while being incredibly simple with easy ingredients). It's imperative, however, that your intent is pure.

INGREDIENTS

White candle
Green candle
Anointing oil blend (see page 17)

INSTRUCTIONS

I. Anoint both candles with the anointing oil blend. Place them 9 inches (23 cm) apart on a table. Keep in mind the white candle represents you, and the green candle represents money.

2. Think of your intent, visualizing money coming in from the universe, then say the incantation.

3. Repeat this spell every day for nine days at the exact same time each day. Move the candles 1 inch (2.5 cm) closer each time the spell is cast. Once the candles are touching, the spell is complete.

INCANTATION

Three times three, money come to me.

Listen to my command, as I say,

Bless me with riches, harming no one on its way.

So mote it be!

Bring me money three times three.

SPELL NOTES:

DATE: _____   TIME: _____

MOON PHASE: _____

RESULTS/MODIFICATIONS: _____

_____

_____

_____

_____

_____

_____

_____

_____

_____

_____

_____

_____

_____

What are three money manifestations or achievements you're grateful for?

What opportunities can you engage in to generate more money?

What are some things that money cannot buy?

Love
Spells

This journal began with spells promoting healing, and now it ends with spells on love. A good deal of emotional healing pertains to matters of the heart, such as grieving, repairing it, and getting to a place where you can move on. Love, however, isn't just about your relationship with others. Remember, you must find ways to love yourself.

Love Thyself Spell Jar

Love spells are popular for bringing back an old lover or finding a new lover. But before you can focus on external love, it's important to find it internally for yourself. Some of us need a little help with that, and this spell jar can assist with inner peace and finding love from within.

INGREDIENTS

Pinch of pink salt

Green aventurine

Pinch of catnip

12 rose petals

5 drops rosemary essential oil

7 drops rose essential oil

Small jar

12 inches (30 cm) of lavender ribbon

INSTRUCTIONS

1. Add the ingredients to a jar in the following order: pink salt, green aventurine, catnip, rose petals, rosemary essential oil, and rose essential oil. Speak the incantation aloud as you add each ingredient.

2. Repeat the step a second time, making sure the jar is full. Screw on the top and tie the ribbon around it.

> Green is the color of the heart chakra, and green aventurine is a great crystal for love in your life, especially self-love. It helps balance your energy, bring objectivity, promote a sense of well-being, and helps open you to give and receive love. This stone works well when placed on your heart chakra or in your left hand while meditating.

INCANTATION

With this pink salt, I pour for renewal of love for myself.
Green aventurine to comfort my heart.
This catnip is for positive energy and happiness.
With these rose petals, I add for peace of mind.
Rosemary oil to purify,
And rose oil to allow me to heal.

SPELL NOTES:

DATE: TIME:

MOON PHASE:

RESULTS/MODIFICATIONS:

What makes you feel loved?

What do you need more of in your love life? Less of?

What's one of the most memorable experiences you've had with love?

A Note for Love

When it comes to love, although you may have someone specific in mind, it's better to visualize specific characteristics you would like in the person. Although love happens best when we aren't looking, it's good to add some positive motivation.

INGREDIENTS

Red candle
Pink pen
Sheet of paper
5 fresh rose petals
Lavender sachet

INSTRUCTIONS

1. Light the candle. Breathe deeply as you stare at the flame and think of your ideal mate.

2. With the pen and paper, write adjectives that describe this person (funny, successful, intelligent, etc.).

3. Take the five rose petals and kiss them one by one, assigning each phrase to a petal: (1) to cherish, (2) to have, (3) to happiness, (4) to passion, (5) to love.

4. Place each petal on the sheet of paper, making sure the petals are touching and slightly overlapping. Gently fold the paper into thirds, being careful not to disturb the petals. Fold it in on itself, so that the edges are sealed.

5. Place the folded paper into the sachet and hold it between your hands as you focus your intention. Once you feel your intention is clear, blow out the candle.

6. Carry the sachet with you wherever you go, but make sure it's concealed so no one but you knows where it is.

SPELL NOTES:

DATE: TIME:

MOON PHASE:

RESULTS/MODIFICATIONS:

Is there someone you're in love with? Why?

_____

_____

_____

_____

What parts of your life would you like to share with someone?

_____

_____

_____

_____

When do you feel most confident in love?

_____

_____

_____

_____

Intimacy Spell

Often spells are used to bring someone new into your life or someone back into your life. But this spell is for someone who's already in your life, and it brings vibrancy and rejuvenation into the relationship to help renew closeness.

INGREDIENTS

¼ teaspoon powdered sugar
Vase of water (rainwater recommended)
Fresh pink rose
Red pen
Sheet of pink paper
Small rose quartz

INSTRUCTIONS

1. Pour the powdered sugar into the vase. Place the rose in the water.

2. Write your name and the name of your mate on the slip of paper in red ink. Fold it neatly and tightly and slip it between the petals of the rose. Place the rose quartz in between a different set of petals.

3. Speak the incantation aloud as you focus on the person and the intimacy you'd like to have with them.

4. Leave the flower until the bud dries and droops. Save the paper and stone, putting them in a sacred place (in a bedside drawer or on a desk), and bury the flower.

CUSTOMIZATION

Instead of a fresh pink rose, you can also use the flower of your choice, one that you not only feel a gravitational pull to but also makes you think of sensuality. Follow your intuition!

INCANTATION

Bring me closer to [PERSON'S NAME].
Bring [PERSON'S NAME] closer to me.
Reignite our passions
And our zest for life and each other.
Blessed be.

SPELL NOTES:

DATE: TIME:

MOON PHASE:

RESULTS/MODIFICATIONS:

Describe your idea of a fulfilling partnership.

What character strengths do you feel you bring to a loving relationship?

In what ways can you cultivate more love in your life and relationships?

Ex-Energy Cleansing Ritual

Just because an ex-lover is gone doesn't mean that remnants of their presence have left your home, your workspace, or even your car. A smoke cleansing ritual like this one can help free you of the lingering effects of their presence.

INGREDIENTS

Incense stick (or loose incense) of choice
Burning bowl (or cauldron)

INSTRUCTIONS

1. Light the incense. With your burning bowl, walk through each room of your home, speaking the incantation. Once complete, put out the smoldering end by dabbing the burning end into the burning bowl.

2. Allow fresh air to enter the area and let the old air out.

CUSTOMIZATION

Before the spell, meditate on the positive memories in your common spaces that have nothing to do with your ex, breathing life into happy memories and positive energies.

INCANTATION

Blessed be,
Allow [NAME]'s energy to leave this place.
With honor to our time together,
I now release their energy from my sacred space,
And look forward to moving forward anew.

SPELL NOTES:

DATE: TIME:

MOON PHASE:

RESULTS/MODIFICATIONS:

Write about the manner in which you wish to move on and what you want out of your next relationship.

_____

_____

_____

_____

Who do you need to eliminate from your life? Who do you need to invite into it?

_____

_____

_____

_____

Make a list of the ways you can emotionally recharge.

_____

_____

_____

_____

Ending Heartbreak

Heartbreak and loss can be represented through many things. For this reason, there are many variations of easing the pain of heartbreak. With this spell, the journey to healing can be made a little shorter.

INGREDIENTS

Blue candle
Green candle
Red candle
White candle
Burning bowl (or cauldron)
Rose incense
White sage smudge stick (or alternative)

INSTRUCTIONS

1. Place the candles in a circular formation, with the burning bowl in the center. Light the candles. Stick the rose incense into, or on the side of, the smudge stick so that they can burn together. Light them and place them in the burning bowl.

2. Think about your heartbreak—the who, what, where, and why. Visualize a dam bursting, water overflowing, representing your emotions. Imagine them being released away from you.

3. Speak the incantation, then blow out the candles one by one. Stub out the smudge stick and rose incense in the burning bowl.

4. Take the burning bowl outside and toss the ashes.

While magick and journaling can be huge factors in your emotional healing journey, it usually takes an average of three months to get over an ex. This is almost the same amount of time it takes to break a habit, which is roughly ten weeks, or two and a half months. Stay strong; time conquers all.

INCANTATION

Three times three—
Let my strength be returned to me.
Let my heartbreak end and leave me,
Cleansed, strong, pure, and free.
With harm to no one come,
Allow my will for this spell to be done.
So mote it be.

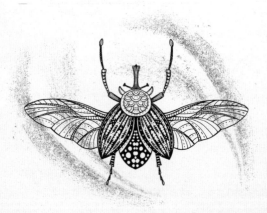

SPELL NOTES:

DATE: TIME:

MOON PHASE:

RESULTS/MODIFICATIONS:

What can best bring you joy during this time?

_____

_____

_____

_____

What has inspired you lately to put your mind elsewhere?

_____

_____

_____

_____

Write a thank you letter to yourself for your strength through this process.

_____

_____

_____

_____

_____

Conclusion

I hope that this journal has been able to help you learn and grow, as well as strengthen your skills at spell casting. As a final note, I would like to leave you with some journal prompts to help you continue your journey, as well as reflect on what you've learned here. Continue to step forward and stand strong.

Blessed be.
—A.G.

How are you better today than you were yesterday?

List your weaknesses and ways to turn them into strengths.

What was the most painful thing you've endured? How did you survive it and what did you learn from it?

Going forward, how will you spend your time?

What do you look forward to learning?

© 2021 by Quarto Publishing Group USA Inc.

First published in 2021 by Wellfleet Press,
an imprint of The Quarto Group
142 West 36th Street, 4th Floor
New York, NY 10018, USA
(212) 779-4972
www.Quarto.com

Wellfleet titles are also available at discount for retail, wholesale, promotional, and bulk purchase. For details, contact the Special Sales Manager by email at specialsales@quarto.com or by mail at The Quarto Group, Attn: Special Sales Manager, 100 Cummings Center Suite 265D, Beverly, MA 01915 USA.

10 9 8 7 6

ISBN: 978-1-57715-242-2

Publisher: Rage Kindelsperger
Creative Director: Laura Drew
Managing Editor: Cara Donaldson
Senior Editor: John Foster
Editorial Assistant: Yashu Pericherla
Cover and Interior Design: Laura Klynstra

Printed in China

For entertainment and educational purposes only. Do not attempt any spell, recipe, procedure, or prescription in this book otherwise. The author, publisher, packager, manufacturer, distributor, and their collective agents waive all liability for the reader's use or application of any of the text herein. Use great caution when working with fire by having plenty of water or a fire extinguisher at the ready.